I0762618

TIME for KiDS

YOUR HOT JOB

FIELD GUIDE

by **Allison Singer**

PENGUIN YOUNG READERS LICENSES
An imprint of Penguin Random House LLC
1745 Broadway, New York, NY 10019
penguinrandomhouse.com

Design by Hsiao-Pin Lin

First published in the United States of America by
Penguin Young Readers Licenses, 2026

Manufactured in China
TOPL

ISBN 9798217143139
10 9 8 7 6 5 4 3 2 1

The authorized representative in the EU for product safety and compliance is Penguin Random House Ireland, Morrison Chambers, 32 Nassau Street, Dublin D02 YH68, Ireland, https://eu-contact.penguin.ie.

. . . .

Photo credits: Cover: Adobe Stock: (beaker) VectorBum; (brushes and palette) Tatiana; (firefighter helmet) anatolir; (gavel) Metaverse; (measuring tape) StudioGraphic; (robot) Ekaterina Karikh; (rocket) Tymofii; (stethoscope) Stockgiu. **Getty Images:** (briefcase, graduation cap) LueratSatichob/DigitalVision Vectors. **Interior: Adobe Stock:** 1: (beaker) VectorBum, (rocket) Tymofii; 10: pressmaster; 13: Lomb; 15: Yistocking; 26: Pixel-Shot; 39: Rido; 40: andreysha74; 44: Seventyfour; 62: David; 66: Shi; 76: Sunny studio; 88: Daniel; 91: Mary Long; 95: pressmaster; 96: Dmitry Kovalchuk; 100: Andrii Oleksiienko; 103: lithiumphoto; 105: deagreez. **Getty Images:** Endpapers, 28: drogatnev/iStock; 1: (basketball) JakeOlimb/DigitalVision Vectors; 5: wenich-mit/iStock; 7: AlonzoDesign/DigitalVision Vectors; 12: vector/iStock; 31: Halfpoint/iStock; 34: Suspended Image/E+; 46: Graphicscoco/E+; 50: mixetto/E+; 53: FatCamera/E+; 55: FG Trade/E+; 56: sturti/E+; 61: Hispanolistic/E+; 68: eatcute/iStock; 69 (notebook) rustemgurler/DigitalVision Vectors, (pencil) Victor_85/iStock; 73: AnnaStills/iStock; 78: Ali Kahfi/DigitalVision Vectors; 79: aleksandarvelasevic/DigitalVision Vectors; 81: Nanci Santos/iStock; 83: South_agency/E+; 84: StockPlanets/E+; 85: FilippoBacci/E+; 93: Devrimb/iStock; 102: bortonia/DigitalVision Vectors.

CONTENTS

INTRODUCTION

Imagine this: You walk into a giant room filled with hundreds, maybe thousands, of doors. Some are tall and heavy-looking. Some are tiny and mysterious. Some are lined with odd materials, such as rulers or paintbrushes. Each door leads to a different path, a different future career. Which do you open first?

Some people grow up knowing exactly which door they want to open. Others have a different approach. They take their time, peeking into many different doors before eventually picking one to try. If they don't like what they find, they try a different option. Slowly they discover the door that is just right for them.

Which door, or career path, is just right for you? While there is no one way to figure it out, the goal of this book is to give you the information you need to start considering your future.

Think of this book as your ultimate guide to the world of work—the jobs people do, what they love about them, and how you can start exploring the kinds of things you

might want to do for your career one day.

Your career path doesn't have to be a straight line. In fact, it probably won't be. It will zig and zag. It will change and evolve. It may even surprise you at times! And it will likely be influenced by the skills, talents, and interests you already have—even the ones that seem like hobbies or just-for-fun activities now.

Maybe you like constructing things out of cardboard or LEGOs. Maybe you're the go-to person in your family when someone's tablet or computer crashes. Maybe you can make your friends laugh with ease, or maybe you're the person classmates seek out when they're feeling lonely. These traits might not seem like they are related to your future career, but they are. The things you excel at are clues—hints about the kinds of unique skills and abilities you're already developing. These clues can help you figure out what careers might make you feel excited, creative, helpful, or proud.

Vocab word: A **CAREER** is the path a person takes through work. It's not just one job—it's a journey made of all the jobs, skills, and professional experiences you collect as you go along.

The world of careers is always evolving. Technology is changing more rapidly than ever before. Jobs that were done one way for decades are now being done in an entirely different way. Many jobs that people have today didn't even exist a few years ago, and new ones are being invented all the time.

In this book, you'll meet people with all kinds of jobs. They spoke with TIME for Kids about what makes their career unique. Some jobs might be familiar to you, such as teachers, chefs, and firefighters. Others, such as flight surgeons and sports team travel coordinators, could be professions that are completely new to you. Within these pages, there are plenty of cutting-edge careers, like cybersecurity professionals and robotics engineers. For each of these and more, you'll get a peek into what the job is really like, what skills it requires, and what you can do today to get started.

Most importantly, this book will help you learn about yourself. In the first chapter, you'll take a quiz called the Skills Explorer. It's from Your Hot Job, a free career-exploration website powered by the editors of TIME for Kids. (I'm one of them—hi!) The quiz will help you uncover your unique skills, talents, and interests. Use your results to start imagining what jobs might one day be a good fit. But if your results don't line up with the future you envision for yourself, that's all right, too. Only *you* have the power to choose your future path.

In later chapters, you'll find out about different industries you can join, the power-ups that can help supercharge your journey, and the obstacles you may need to overcome. At the end of each chapter, you'll find activities that will help you think about all you've learned and expand on key concepts.

As you read, the most important thing to remember is this: You don't have to have your whole future figured out right now. What matters most is being curious, asking questions, trying new things, and paying attention to what makes you feel energized and confident. That's how you start to build a life, and a career, that's just right for you.

So, whether you're someone who doodles in the margins of your notebook, enjoys organizing their backpack, is always brimming with big ideas, or prefers museums to movies, there's a career path where you can shine.

There are an unlimited number of different paths to success. Some people go to college or graduate school, or beyond; some learn through apprenticeships or job training; others jump right into work or start their own business. Your career journey can be as unique as you are. Be brave enough to try new things. Ask questions. Listen closely. Pay attention to what makes you feel excited or inspired.

Ready to begin the adventure? There's a whole world of careers out there. Let's peek behind the first door and see where it leads.

CHAPTER 1

LOOK INSIDE

Before you can figure out where you're going, you have to know who you are.

Everyone has different strengths. People also have different interests and ways of thinking. Some people love solving puzzles. Others enjoy helping their community, imagining new worlds, or tinkering with machines until they work just right. There's no one "best" skill or personality type. Knowing who you are is more than knowing what you like or what your best school subject is. But the more you know about what you're naturally good at or drawn to, the more confident you'll feel as you start thinking about future career paths.

Sometimes, a career might spark your interest that involves a subject or skill that is more challenging to you. Don't be discouraged! Just because a skill doesn't come easily right away doesn't mean you can't work hard to build it over time. Remember: Having passion for your future job is key, so don't avoid a career you're passionate about just because you doubt your skills.

The quiz in this chapter is designed to help you reflect on what lights you up. You'll answer 36 questions about things you like, how you approach problems, and how different situations make you feel. Once you've answered them all, you'll total up your results and learn about six traits that describe the ways people work, think, and thrive. You'll find out which traits show up most strongly for you and how they might connect to real careers.

This quiz won't tell you exactly what job you should do. (Sorry! There's no magical machine for that.) But it will give you clues. Your reaction to those clues—what feels right, what makes you say "that sounds like me"—can point you in the right direction.

So grab a separate piece of paper and a pen or pencil, and get ready to explore. Be honest with your answers. Be curious about your results. And, most importantly, be open to discovering something new about yourself.

Tip: The Skills Explorer quiz is also available online, with extended results. Check it out at timeforkids.com/your-hot-job.

Skills Explorer

On a separate sheet of paper, rank each of the following statements from 1 (definitely not me) to 5 (totally me).

1. I enjoy learning how to fix things, such as a bike.
2. I like doing science experiments.
3. I would enjoy designing my own clothes.
4. I like tutoring or teaching others.
5. I like selling things.
6. I like things organized and clean.
7. I like to put things together, such as LEGO kits.
8. I like solving complex math problems.
9. I enjoy sketching, drawing, or painting.
10. I like volunteering at school and in my community.
11. I dream of owning a small business.
12. I am detail-oriented.
13. I like to be outdoors.
14. I like dreaming up new inventions.
15. I like to take pictures of everything.

16. I like talking in front of people.
17. I like competing at school or sports.
18. I like having clear instructions to follow.
19. I like taking care of animals.
20. I'm a curious person by nature.
21. I like to sing or play an instrument.
22. I enjoy leading discussions.
23. I finish the projects I start.
24. I like keeping lists.
25. I'm good at figuring out how things work.
26. I like using new technology.
27. I like writing stories or poems.
28. I like making new friends.
29. I like learning about money.
30. I am a rule-follower.
31. I like to cook.
32. I like to be challenged.
33. I like to use my imagination.
34. I like trying to help people solve their problems.
35. I like setting goals for myself.
36. I enjoy working on the computer.

Results

To get your Skills Explorer results, total up your scores for each of the six colors. The color with the highest score is your **leading** trait. Start by finding that trait's description on pages 19–24. Does it sound like you? What feels spot-on? What doesn't?

Then, look at the color with your second-highest score. This is your **supporting** trait.

Finally, read through the rest of the traits in the order you ranked them. You might find pieces of yourself in more than just the top two. That's totally normal. Almost everyone is a unique mix of all six traits.

Keep your top two traits in mind as you read the rest of this book. But remember: This quiz is just a starting point. It's here to help you begin thinking about your skills, talents, interests, and passions. Your results on this quiz, or any other quiz, don't define you; most people will agree with their results in some places but not in others. In the end, only you can decide what fits and where you want to go next.

Realistic: You get things done.

This means: You know what's up. You care about the things that have a real impact on your life. Other people worry about abstract ideas and hypothetical situations. But not you! You value what's real: the things you can see, touch, and use.

Your superpowers are: Never-ending curiosity about how things work, and the courage to dig in and find out.

You may be: Athletic. Independent. Practical. Ambitious.

You may enjoy: Being in nature. Working with your hands. Competition.

Careers to consider: Solar-panel installer (page 38). Animal service worker (page 58). Auto mechanic.

Investigative: You think things through.

• • •

This means: You observe the world with a keen eye. You're eager to ask questions—and you love finding answers. When faced with a problem, you aren't satisfied until you've thought of a solution. Your brain can do some pretty amazing things.

Your superpowers are: Thinking, observing, and making sense of tricky concepts and situations.

You may be: Curious. Cautious. Independent. Dedicated.

You may enjoy: Being challenged. Exploring new ideas. Researching.

Careers to consider: Software engineer (page 32). Judge (page 63). Astrophysicist (page 36).

Artistic: You love to create.

This means: Go ahead, express yourself! You get excited about creative projects. When you unleash your imagination, there's no telling where it will take you. And you've got what it takes to bring your creation to life, whether it's a poem or digital artwork.

Your superpowers are: Using your imagination and creativity to lead the way; finding beauty in a messy world.

You may be: Creative. Imaginative. Innovative. Bold.

You may enjoy: Talent shows. Abstract thinking. Working independently.

Careers to consider: Video-game designer (page 52). Landscape architect (page 38). Drone operator (page 33).

Social: You're here to help.

This means: You shine brightest when surrounded by friends and family. When you see someone struggling, you have a deep desire to help. The world needs more people like you. When you have a concern, you jump into action.

Your superpowers are: Getting along with just about everybody and making others feel at ease.

You may be: Helpful. Outgoing. Understanding. Insightful.

You may enjoy: Working in groups. Lively discussions. Helping people.

Careers to consider: Physical therapist. Educator. Flight attendant (page 60).

Enterprising: You have persuasive powers.

• • •

This means: You loved being line leader in kindergarten, didn't you? Being enterprising means you like to be in charge, and you're probably good at it. It also means you like working with others and have strong speaking and presenting skills.

Your superpowers are: Being confident in your ideas, and convincing others you know the way to go.

You may be: Adventurous. Confident. Ambitious. Inquisitive.

You may enjoy: Explaining things. Giving presentations. Organizing events.

Careers to consider: Entrepreneur (page 47). Software engineer (page 32). Lawyer.

Conventional: You keep it all organized.

This means: You care about details. Numbers, data, facts: You're on top of it all. Do you have an organizational system for your notes? Categorized music playlists? We wouldn't be surprised. You just like things to make sense.

Your superpowers are: Staying focused and keeping others focused when following rules or instructions.

You may be: Organized. Ambitious. Efficient. Responsible.

You may enjoy: Playing board games. Reading books. Collecting things.

Careers to consider: Aircraft technician. Sports statistician (page 80). Librarian.

Activity 1

You've just completed the Skills Explorer quiz and gotten your results. That's a lot to digest! Write down your thoughts about the results. What intrigued you? What surprised you?

16 940
Home apartment
1000
10000
10000
23 040
17 800
8700
15 800
1000

CHAPTER 2

FIND YOUR FIELD

An industry is a group of related jobs. People in the same industry often work toward a common goal, such as improving health, solving environmental issues, or designing useful technology. There are many different industries. Each one includes a wide mix of roles.

You might already have an ability that you've sharpened (skill), a topic that you're passionate about (interest), or something that you're naturally good at (talent). These are great starting points. But the same starting points can lead to totally different careers, in completely different industries. Let's say you're great at math and love baseball; you could become a sports analyst, invent new athletic equipment, or code the next hit sports video game. Maybe you care about animals and are fascinated by machines; some tech careers focus on creating tools to track or protect endangered wildlife, while some careers in hands-on animal care use cutting-edge technology to heal animals. Your skills, interests, and talents can take you in more directions than you might expect.

You don't have to choose just one part of yourself when deciding on a potential future career. Your skills, interests, and talents are all ingredients in the recipe that make up your very unique self—and all of them will help you explore your many options.

There's no single way to turn what you love into what you do. That's why this chapter introduces a wide range of industries. Each section includes a short overview of the industry, plus real examples of jobs within it. You'll meet people doing that work right now, hear what they love about it, and get a glimpse of what the future might hold.

Tip: For each industry, you'll find examples of three hot jobs. These roles are in high demand and expected to grow in the coming years. Curious about other careers? Visit the Your Hot Job website (see page 104) to explore more options through articles, interviews, and videos. You can even earn digital badges as you go.

As you read, think about where your skills, interests, and talents could fit. Keep an open mind: Your "dream" job might be one you haven't heard of yet—or a job that *no one* has. In a 2016 World Economic Forum report, experts wrote that 65 percent of children entering primary school that year will likely grow up to have jobs that didn't yet exist. How do you prepare for a career that won't be possible for another 20 or 30 years? We'll get to that. (Or, if you want to skip ahead, turn to page 68!) For now, explore the following industries, and imagine the possibilities.

Technology

Technology is everywhere—in classrooms, in hospitals, on farms, in outer space. It powers the tools people use, the ways we connect and share information, and the systems that keep our world running. That's why career paths in the technology industry are some of the most exciting and fast-changing.

People in tech build hardware, write software, protect data, and solve problems that affect countless lives. Some people design apps or websites. Others work on robots, satellites, or cybersecurity systems. Many jobs in this field focus on innovation. That means finding ways to do things faster, smarter, or more safely.

Technology plays a role in every other industry in this book, with no exceptions. It lets scientists track climate data, helps auto mechanics maintain and repair cars, allows doctors to diagnose illnesses, and supports artists and designers in bringing their ideas to life. Tech skills can take you in almost any direction.

If you like coding, gaming, or building, or you're curious about how things work, you might find your future career in tech. It's a place for creative problem solvers, systematic thinkers, and dedicated learners who want to help crack the code to the future.

THREE HOT JOBS IN TECH:

- **SOFTWARE ENGINEERS** write code that powers technology, including computer programs and devices. They work on everything from social media to medical tools. It may seem like a solitary gig, but software engineers value collaboration. YouTube engineer Miles Hinson says, "If someone made a mistake in their code or did something that is a little confusing, another person can ask them questions or point out those mistakes."
- **CYBERSECURITY ANALYSTS** protect computer systems from hackers and other threats.

They monitor networks, investigate attacks, and find new ways to keep information safe. Kayley Kish is a cyber threat intelligence analyst. She pays close attention to detail. "Even the smallest bit of information can make a big difference with your analysis," Kish says.

- **DRONE OPERATORS** remotely pilot drones to perform tasks and capture images from above. Nikolai Zychowicz captures images for social media, TV, and film. Like all commercial drone operators, he has to study for and pass a test administered by the Federal Aviation Administration every two years to keep his license. "You have to know how to read flight paths, maps, and airspaces, and what all of the markings mean," Zychowicz says.

Space

Space is vast, mysterious, and full of possibility. It's also a growing industry right here on Earth. People who work in space-related careers are launching satellites, studying other planets, building spacecraft, and exploring the universe.

The space industry includes scientists, engineers, pilots, technicians, and more. Of course, it also includes astronauts—but most space jobs happen in labs, offices, and mission control centers on this planet.

As technology advances, careers in the space industry are becoming more accessible. You could be designing space suits, researching black holes, or analyzing soil from Mars. How about a job as a space journalist, space photographer, or space chef? The options are limitless.

THREE HOT SPACE JOBS:

- **AEROSPACE ENGINEERS** design aircraft, spacecraft, and satellites. Their work helps people travel to space, send data across the globe, and learn about the universe. Joan Melendez Misner is an aerospace integration engineer at NASA. "As a young girl, I looked at the stars," she says. "I'd always be fascinated by what was out in outer space."

- **FLIGHT SURGEONS** are doctors who provide care for pilots. They specialize in knowing how flight can affect a person's body. As a flight surgeon at NASA, Dr. David Picken cares for astronauts. "It's a pretty cool job to help get someone ready to fly to space, take care of them while they're out there, and see them when they come home," he says.
- **ASTROPHYSICISTS** study planets, stars, and other celestial bodies. Some study distant galaxies and phenomena such as black holes. Others monitor space debris. "You open up your mind to everything that's out there in the universe," astrophysicist Jackie Faherty says, "and you start studying stuff that will help bring you closer to getting those kinds of answers."

Climate

Careers in the climate industry focus on protecting the environment and making the future more sustainable. People in this field work to understand weather patterns, develop clean energy sources, conserve natural habitats, and educate others on environmental issues. Some are scientists studying the atmosphere. Others are engineers building eco-friendly technologies. There are also advocates, educators, and leaders raising awareness and inspiring action.

If you care about nature, enjoy science class, or feel strongly about solving real-world problems, a career in the climate industry might be right for you. It's a field that values curiosity, passion, and dedication to protecting the planet.

THREE HOT JOBS IN CLIMATE:

- **ATMOSPHERIC SCIENTISTS** research the weather and climate. Some are meteorologists who report the weather to the public. Ashley Ruiz works as a television meteorologist. "Meeting the families who saw the forecast and were able to get to safety—it's amazing, knowing I helped make that happen," she says.

- **SOLAR-PANEL INSTALLERS** assemble, set up, and maintain rooftop panels that turn sunlight into energy. This job is really heating up; the need for solar-panel installers is expected to see big growth in the coming years. "As an electrician by trade," says Frank Curran, "I saw solar as a way to use my electrical talents to do something positive for the environment and the future of the planet."
- **LANDSCAPE ARCHITECTS** design parks and outdoor spaces. They choose what plants, trees, and flowers to use, and create the overall design. In other words, they construct everything outside of buildings. "You might call us architects of the earth," says landscape architect Pamela Conrad.

Agriculture

When most people hear the word *agriculture*, they think of farms. This isn't wrong! Agriculture is the industry that grows the food we eat and the plants we use for things such as clothing, fuel, and medicine. But there's more to it.

Today's agriculture industry combines science, technology, and problem-solving to grow food in smarter, more sustainable ways. People in agriculture work with

plants and animals, as well as with data, robotics, and environmental systems. Some are working in factories and labs. Some are using drones to study crops from above. And, yes, many still get their hands dirty digging in the dirt (and love doing it!).

Agriculture is a career path where you can make a real impact. As the global population grows, we'll need more food—grown using fewer resources. Climate change, soil health, and water conservation are just a few of the major challenges people in this industry are working to solve.

If you're interested in nature, science, animals, climate, or food, this industry is worth exploring. It's full of roles for doers, innovators, and caretakers. Whether you want to be outside in the field or inside in a lab, there's room to grow your career in agriculture.

THREE HOT JOBS IN AGRICULTURE:

- **FOOD SCIENTISTS** find ways to make food better and safer. They work in labs and perform tests on both raw and processed foods. They also help companies create new products and improve existing ones. Ice-cream scientist Maya Warren describes the job as "incredibly intriguing." "It's very much a passion," she adds, "but it's also a desire for knowledge."
- **AGRICULTURAL TECHNICIANS** keep farms up and running. They collect data, conduct experiments, and maintain equipment. They also play an important role in implementing

new agricultural methods and technologies. They work in all kinds of conditions: "It could be snowing and below zero, or 108 degrees with a brisk 40-mile-per-hour wind," says service technician Nick Helton.

- **ORGANIC FARMERS** grow food without synthetic chemicals, and with a focus on sustainability and soil health. This career draws people from many different backgrounds. "Farming caught my attention," says Mia Tramz, who transitioned to farming after a corporate career in media. "There are endless things to learn."

Health

The health industry is all about helping people feel their best. It includes a wide range of careers that focus on caring for the body and mind. From treating illnesses to promoting wellness, health professionals play a vital role in our communities and world.

Some health workers, such as doctors and nurses, provide direct care. Others work behind the scenes, conducting research, managing data, or developing new treatments. There are also roles focused on prevention and education.

Many health jobs require extra years of schooling. They also require patience and collaboration. Strong judgment is important, too.

THREE HOT JOBS IN HEALTH:

- **PEDIATRICIANS** are doctors who specialize in caring for kids. They treat illnesses, conduct checkups, and help kids stay healthy. Dr. Johanna Rodriguez-Toledo was the first in her family to graduate from college. "Even though it is hard work," she says, "it is worth it to make a difference in the lives of kids."

- **CERTIFIED REGISTERED NURSE ANESTHETISTS** (CRNAs) are nurses who administer anesthesia during surgeries. They keep patients comfortable and safe. CRNA Brett Hayes says, "If you want an exciting career with direct, hands-on caring for people and saving lives, you won't regret picking anesthesia."
- **MEDICAL RESEARCHERS** study diseases and search for new treatments. Their work helps improve public health and can lead to life-saving discoveries. "Viruses move very fast," says Gavin Cloherty, who leads a group of experts dedicated to fighting pandemic diseases. "We also need to be moving very fast."

Business

Every time your family buys a snack, watches a commercial, or uses an app or computer program, they're interacting with a product or service that started as someone's idea. Business is the industry that turns those ideas into reality and figures out how to make them successful.

People who work in business help companies plan and grow. Some start businesses of their own. Others work in marketing, sales, finance, or management. They solve problems, lead teams, study data, and look for efficient ways to get things done. It's a field that rewards bravery, creativity, and strategic thinking.

Business careers can be fast-paced. They are ever-changing. They often involve setting goals, collaborating with others, and making little decisions that affect the big picture. Many jobs in this field rely on strong math, writing, and communication skills.

To build a career in this industry, you'll need to move fast and be flexible. If you enjoy coming up with ideas, solving puzzles, or leading group projects, a career in business could be a great fit.

THREE HOT JOBS IN BUSINESS:

- **ENTREPRENEURS** start their own businesses. They spot opportunities, take risks, and build something from the ground up. Beauty entrepreneur Michelle Phan was the first woman to build a $500 million company from a web series. Entrepreneurs "have to see potential in something that no one is looking at," she says.
- **FUNDRAISERS** work to help companies and organizations raise money. They plan events, organize drives, and do outreach to potential donors. But Ivan Adames of the Chicago Botanic Garden notes that his job as a fundraiser is really about "more than dollars." He also persuades people to donate their time and professional expertise, which he

says "have tremendous value."

- **BUYERS** are responsible for the selection of goods you see in a store. They track trends, research vendors, and test items on shelves to see how customers react. Brian Winters is a buyer for a large chain of grocery stores. He encourages all employees to come to him with exciting ideas. "My door is always open," Winters says.

Creators

Creators shape the way people see the world. They tell stories, design experiences, and express ideas through words, images, sound, and movement. From books and movies to video games, podcasts, and graphic design, creators work across many different mediums.

This industry includes writers, artists, designers, performers, and media makers. Some work behind the scenes, while others shine in the spotlight. Some build careers as employees at big companies, and others work independently as entrepreneurs, or as freelancers who sell their services. What unites them is their ability to imagine something new and bring it to life.

Vocab word: A **FREELANCER** is a worker who can sell their services to multiple companies or groups at once. Freelancers work in every industry and offer a variety of skills, from web design and coding to makeup artistry and accounting. What makes freelancers unique is that they are self-employed; they take on projects with individual clients rather than making a long-term commitment to one employer.

Creative careers rely on strong communication skills, curiosity, and the ability to look at things from a fresh angle. These jobs can be highly collaborative; writers might work with editors, illustrators with art directors, and performers with stage or video production teams. While the work is often fun and exciting, it also requires discipline and persistence.

If you enjoy drawing, writing, performing, filming, editing, or inventing stories and characters, this could be a path worth exploring. The tools might change—new technology is always opening up new possibilities—but the need for creative thinkers will never go out of style.

THREE HOT CREATOR JOBS:

- **PODCAST PRODUCERS** bring stories to life, in your ears. They plan episodes, oversee recording sessions, and edit the final file. Some work on interviews, while others build narrative shows with music and sound effects. It's part tech, part storytelling, and all about keeping listeners invested. Podcast producer Christie Taylor says that she often finds herself asking, "What does the audience want to hear?"

- **VIDEO-GAME DESIGNERS** and developers imagine and build the games people love to play. They come up with characters, environments, and visual effects that make games immersive and exciting. Mitu Khandaker started her own game-development company. "The best game designers are people who have a really wide range of interests," she says. "You want to bring those into games."
- **STORYBOARD ARTISTS** sketch out the action for animated TV shows and movies. They create a visual outline of the important moments in a story, often turning text into images. Jackie Bae has served as a storyboard artist for many well-known TV shows. "Growing up, I loved drawing and cartoons," she says. "I never grew out of doodling on the back of my homework. So that was where it started."

Sports

You already know that professional athletes have careers in sports. But they're only one part of the big picture. Behind every game is a whole team of people who make sports possible, from coaches and athletic trainers to statisticians and marketing pros.

The sports industry includes jobs in health, media, hospitality, and business. Some people work with athletes to help them improve their skills or stay in top physical and mental shape. Others promote events, study game data, or manage operations for teams. Some sports careers involve travel. Others are based in schools, gyms, or offices.

This is an industry driven by passion. Sports jobs can be

fast-paced and demanding, but also rewarding—especially if you love the energy of competition and working with a team. It's a great field for people who are active, organized, and motivated to help others succeed. Are you ready to get in the game?

THREE HOT JOBS IN SPORTS:

- **ATHLETIC TRAINERS** help prevent and treat injuries in athletes. They work in training rooms, in hospitals or clinics, and on the sidelines at games. Their job is to keep athletes healthy and ready to compete. "An athletic trainer is my best friend," says former NFL linebacker Brandon Copeland. "They are making sure my body stays in tip-top shape."
- **TEAM TRAVEL MANAGERS** help coordinate transportation, lodging, and schedules. They make sure the team gets where it needs to go, with all it needs to succeed. "I've always loved to travel, and sports have had a massive impact on my life," says Brynnan Norris, a travel coordinator for the Savannah Bananas. (They're a baseball exhibition team based in Georgia.) "I learned I could combine those two passions into a full-time career."

- **SPORTS REPORTERS** cover games and interview athletes and coaches. They work for newspapers, magazines, TV stations, and websites. Sean Gregory, senior sports correspondent for TIME, has written about famous athletes such as LeBron James and Caitlin Clark. It's a fun gig, he says, but he takes it seriously: "You're not just going to sporting events to cheer. You have a job to do."

Personal Service

Personal service careers involve working closely with individuals to meet their personal needs, whether this means helping someone look their best, stay healthy, or feel supported and safe.

People in personal service roles work in salons, gyms, homes, and on the go. Some jobs, such as hairstylists or

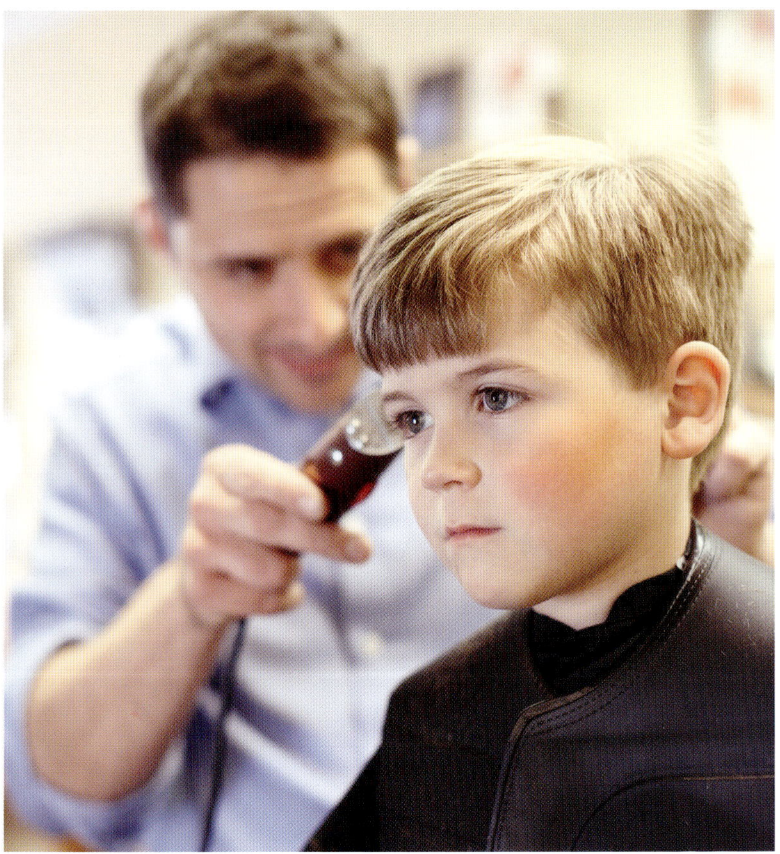

makeup artists, focus on beauty and grooming. There are also roles that provide care and companionship, like childcare workers or personal aides. Tradespeople, such as plumbers and installers, use their specialized training and knowledge to help people keep their homes running.

If you enjoy helping others feel good, whether it's through a fresh haircut, a fun workout, or assistance on a tricky task, the personal service industry may be where you belong. These jobs often require strong people skills, patience, and a genuine desire to make a positive impact on someone's day.

THREE HOT JOBS IN PERSONAL SERVICE:

- **BARBERS** and **HAIRSTYLISTS** cut and style people's hair. They may work for a barbershop or salon, or they may be self-employed. When Darrius Peace decided on a career as a hairstylist, he didn't know where to start; there were no YouTube tutorials in the 1990s! "I just took matters into my own hands and practiced braiding my hair," he says. "It was months and months of trial and error sessions, and then eventually I got it."
- **NUTRITIONISTS** and **DIETICIANS** help people live healthy lives. They may teach someone

how to read menus and food labels, or help them reach a wellness goal. Nutritionists do this work in schools, homes, hospitals, and long-term care facilities. "I get to 'play' with my food when I'm testing and making a recipe," nutritionist Ellie Krieger says. "It's part of my job, and it never gets old."

- **ANIMAL SERVICE WORKERS** care for and train animals. They work in zoos, shelters, clinics, and homes—essentially, anywhere animals live. Dog trainer Shir Limazati typically conducts one-on-one sessions during the week. "I spend my weekends studying all their information so that I'm ready," she says.

Hospitality

The hospitality industry is all about making people feel welcome and cared for. Whether it's helping guests enjoy a vacation, organizing a special event, or serving a delicious meal, hospitality professionals create experiences that people remember.

This field includes a variety of roles, from hotel managers and café owners to event planners and flight attendants. Some work behind the scenes, while others interact directly with guests. What they all share is an attention to detail and a commitment to excellent service.

If you enjoy helping others, solving problems, and creating enjoyable experiences, the hospitality industry will welcome you with open arms.

THREE HOT JOBS IN HOSPITALITY:

- **RESTAURANT MANAGERS**, or **FOOD SERVICE MANAGERS**, are responsible for the operation of restaurants or other places that prepare and serve food and beverages. They direct staff and make sure things run smoothly. Customer service is a big part of this job, says Juan Perez, who manages four rock-and-roll-themed restaurants in California. "You have the power to make the customer's experience unique," he says. "That's one of the things I love most."

- **FLIGHT ATTENDANTS** provide routine services and respond to emergencies to ensure the comfort and safety of airline passengers. They demonstrate the use of safety equipment and take care of people's needs. "As a kid, I used to sit right in the window seat," remembers international flight attendant Jenessa Andrea. "I loved air travel."
- **EVENT PLANNERS** arrange all aspects of special events and professional gatherings. They set meeting locations and coordinate catering, transportation, and other details. On the day of a big event, the most important thing is "keeping your cool," says event planner Andrea Caldwell, "and finding solutions quickly."

Public Service

Public service careers are all about making a positive impact on communities and society as a whole. These jobs often involve working for the government, nonprofit organizations, or educational institutions. Whether it's through creating laws, managing emergencies, educating future generations, or advocating for community needs, public service professionals are dedicated to making the world a better place.

People in public service roles work in various settings, from courtrooms and government offices to schools and libraries. Many of these careers involve assisting people directly, while others focus on systems and policies that affect entire communities.

If you enjoy problem-solving, want to help others, and care about issues affecting your community, you may feel satisfied by a career in public service. These jobs often require strong communication and collaboration skills, as well as a passion for leading the way.

THREE HOT JOBS IN PUBLIC SERVICE:

- **JUDGES** oversee courtrooms and legal matters. They act as referees, ensuring trials are conducted fairly and that both sides operate according to the law. "You can't play favorites," district court judge Karen Sage says. "I'm mostly letting the lawyers try their cases and making sure they follow all the rules correctly. If I've done that, then the right outcome should happen."
- **EMERGENCY MANAGEMENT SPECIALISTS** help communities prepare for and respond to disasters, such as hurricanes and pandemics. This job requires strong organizational skills

and a dedication to public safety. It also requires quick thinking. Jerica Shackelford has more than 20 years of experience in emergency management. "I deal with various challenges in my job, engaging in complex problem-solving regularly," she says. "The most exciting part of the job is that it keeps me on my toes."

- **LOCAL REPRESENTATIVES** are government workers who represent their community's interests. They draft and vote on laws, address community concerns, and work to improve the quality of life for people in their area. "I will fight for my constituents, because they're like my extended family," says New York State Representative Latrice Walker. "I'm accountable to the people who put me in office."

Activity 2

Which three industries interest you most? Write them down and explain what grabs your attention. Maybe it's the type of work, the people it helps, or the skills it puts to use. Now take it a step further: What changes might those industries go through in the next 10 to 15 years? How might new technology change the way in which the work gets done? What new jobs might be needed? Thinking about the future helps you stay open-minded and ready for a career that might not even exist—yet!

CHAPTER 3

CHART A COURSE

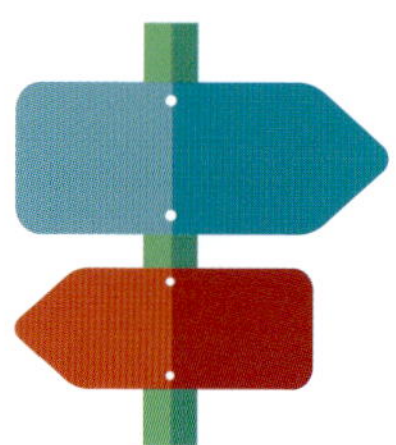

Maybe you already have a dream job in mind. Maybe you don't. Either way, you're in the right place. Choosing a career path can seem like a huge decision, but you don't have to figure it all out right now. In fact, most adults change their minds, and their jobs, multiple times. Remember, your future isn't a straight line. It's more like a winding path, full of new discoveries and surprises.

Want proof? Check this out, from career strategist Terina Allen: "I started with fast-food jobs at Taco Bell and McDonald's when I was a teenager. Then I became an office assistant and a social worker. After that, I decided to become a high school teacher and a college instructor, prior to becoming a management consultant. Many years later, I started my own company. I hired consultants to help me work with clients all over the world. And now, I also write about career and leadership development. Look at how different some of my career experiences have been. I got to choose my own path. You get to choose your own path too."

The first and most important step in choosing that path is being curious and paying attention. Pay attention to what interests you, what challenges you, and what makes you feel like your best self. There are clues all around you—in

Everyone has skills, talents, and interests to explore. One way to do this is by keeping a Future Career Journal. It doesn't have to be fancy—just a notebook or a notes app on a phone or tablet will do. When something catches your attention, excites you, or makes you feel proud, write it down. When you try something new, make a note of how it felt. You can also collect words, drawings, job titles, or quotes that inspire you. It's your journal—make it yours. Over time, you'll start to see patterns that might lead you toward the right career for you.

your hobbies, your favorite classes, your conversations, the shows or games you like. Your job now is to notice those clues and follow where they lead.

Reading this book is a great start. It might give you good ideas for your future. But you won't really know what something is like until you try it. You don't have to wait until you're older to start exploring your potential career paths. There are ways to test your skills, talents, and interests right now. You could:

- Join a new club at school. What's a topic that you're curious to know more about?
- Help a family member with their work. Could you shadow them around their office or workplace for a day?
- Volunteer at a local organization, such as an animal shelter or a community center. What types of jobs are people doing there?
- Sign up for a new class or camp. Do you have a talent you'd like to explore?
- Try a new hobby at home. Will a friend or family member join you?

Experiences like these can help you build skills, meet people, and learn more about what you like. It's all part of the process of choosing your path.

Activity 3

Write down five things you want to try in the next year that could relate to future careers. They can be big things, such as trying out for a new sports team, or small ones, like experimenting with a new cupcake recipe. Circle one to start with. Set a date to try it, and afterward, write down what you learned. Did you learn anything that might help you figure out where your future career path could lead?

The world is full of people who want to help you succeed. Some are mentors. You might find them at school, in your community, or through family. A parent or teacher can also help you search online for people who have the type of career you may be interested in one day.

Vocab word: A **MENTOR** is someone who shares their knowledge and experience to help guide you toward a goal. They might give advice, answer questions, or just listen when you need to talk something through. Mentors can be teachers, coaches, family members, neighbors—anyone who helps you learn and grow.

DeVanté Starks leads a mentorship nonprofit in New Orleans, Louisiana. "No one knows everything, and it's okay to admit you need help," he advises. "If you never ask questions, you'll never get the answers you need. Find someone whom you can look to for guidance and encouragement. Finding a sincere mentee-mentor relationship is one of the best things you can do for your life and [future] career."

An adult doesn't have to be your official "mentor" to share what they know. With a parent's permission, when you meet someone with an interesting job, you can ask if

you can shadow them, help out, or keep in touch. Most people are happy to talk—especially when they see that you're genuinely interested. And remember, the more questions you ask, the more you'll learn. Ask questions like:

- What do you do each day?
- What do you like most about your work?
- What about your work do you find most challenging?
- How did you get started?
- What skills are most important for your job?

Some careers require years of study. Others require hands-on training or a special license. Some jobs you can only learn by doing them. No matter what path you choose, learning will be part of it.

Education doesn't have to mean a four-year college.

It might mean trade school, apprenticeships, certification programs, or online classes. The important thing is to find the kind of learning that works for you and helps you reach your goals.

Curious minds build strong careers. So keep reading, asking questions, practicing new skills, and challenging yourself. You're training your brain to solve problems, think creatively, and work with others—skills that will help in any job.

You might change your mind about what you want to do. That's normal. It doesn't mean you failed. It means you learned something new about yourself.

Many adults switch careers. Some go back to school. Some create a new job that better fits their current skill set. Some start their own business. The most important thing, at any age, is to stay open and keep learning.

You don't have to know your final destination. You're already on your way. You just have to take the next step, and then the next one, until you've built a path that feels like your own unique version of success. Here's career strategist Terina Allen again, with great advice: "If you remember only one thing, remember this: You get to decide the best career path for your life. You get to choose. There is no right or wrong choice. There are many different options, and you get to decide your own best path."

Activity 4

Choose someone who has a career that is interesting to you. Maybe they have your dream job or work in an industry you find intriguing. Research this person and their career. Then, in addition to the example questions suggested earlier in this chapter on page 73, prepare five thoughtful questions tailored to their unique journey. Interview them in person, by phone, or over a video call. Write down what you learn. Pro tip: Don't forget to thank them for their time!

CHAPTER 4

POWER UP

This chapter is about skills that will help you advance on your career path, no matter which direction you're headed. You might hear about types of skills called *soft skills*. Around here, we call them power skills. They're personal, flexible, and power up your ability to succeed in just about every profession.

Unlike specific technical skills—such as coding, plumbing, or writing—power skills are harder to measure. You won't always find them listed in a job description, but they're just as important. They include things like communication, creativity, and problem-solving. These skills take time and experience to build, but they'll serve you in every role you take on. Ready to explore the top eight power skills you'll need on your career journey? Let's dive in.

POWER SKILL: COMMUNICATION

Whether you're writing an essay, giving a presentation, or explaining the rules of a board game, communication is all about making sure your thoughts are shared clearly. This power skill is essential in the workplace. Communication is key for nurses who explain treatment to patients, as well as for sneaker designers who pitch new ideas. Good communicators listen as well as speak: "The most valuable advice I've received is to listen to the guests and don't rush," says hotel concierge Juliet Markowitz. "It's important to get complete information in order to deliver excellent service."

POWER SKILL: FLEXIBILITY

Plans change. A group member gets sick the day of the class presentation. The team's schedule shifts after a game's rained out. Flexibility means staying calm and adjusting as things evolve. The more flexible you are, the more you can handle whatever comes your way. Erika McNab, a program coordinator for the Boulder Chamber of Commerce, says her job requires being "on your feet, pivoting" at every turn. And Gil Bransford stays flexible in his role as an ESPN sports statistician. No two games are ever the same: "With each game," he says, "there's a different story to tell."

POWER SKILL: TIME MANAGEMENT

Time management means knowing what needs to be done and making a plan to do it—even when you'd rather be doing something else. Say you're juggling homework, soccer practice, and a birthday party. Prioritizing helps you fit it all in. In a job, this might look like a construction manager keeping a building project on schedule without cutting critical corners, or an accountant or auditor figuring out how to balance their clients' monthly needs. TFK Kid Reporter Abhijay Potluri interviewed editors at a book-publishing company. "Editors often work under tight deadlines," he later wrote, "so time-management skills are key."

Vocab word: PRIORITIZING means figuring out what's most important to get done and doing that first. It requires understanding how much time needs to be spent on certain things, and knowing the difference between needs versus wants. Students learn to prioritize as they balance family, friends, school, and hobbies.

POWER SKILL: PROBLEM-SOLVING

Not every problem has a quick fix. That's where problem-solving comes in. Lost your tap shoe the day before a dance recital? You'll need to think fast and find a solution. In the working world, this skill helps a set decorator deal with a broken piece of furniture, or a press officer keep a speech on track when the teleprompter goes awry. "If you enjoy problem-solving, you may enjoy a job in design and engineering," suggests entrepreneur Amy Brown. "Being a designer means that the thing you're making may not have any instructions, and you have to figure it out." And when electrician Yordanys Torres arrives at a service call, he uses problem-solving to figure out the issue before fixing it. "It's really the most complex work in the field," he says, "because you never know what you're going to find."

POWER SKILL: ORGANIZATION

Being organized helps you keep track of your things, your thoughts, and your to-do list. Color-coding notes, using checklists, or keeping a tidy desk are all forms of organization. In the workplace, this skill matters for chefs planning kitchen prep, teachers keeping track of student progress, or reporters managing interview notes. During

her time as a fashion product developer, Marrisa Wilson produced items "in a way that was cost-effective and made sense logistically," she says. "If you're someone who's organized . . . then product development is an aspect of fashion you might be interested in."

POWER SKILL: LEADERSHIP

Leadership isn't about being bossy or talking down to your peers. It's about bringing out the best in others. Maybe you take the lead in a class project, helping everyone stay on track and feel included. In a job, leadership might mean managing a team at a tech company or coaching new employees at a restaurant so dinner service goes off without a hitch. Photographer and visual artist Trevor Stuurman defines being a leader as "someone that has a clear point of view, and someone that has a power to inspire." Executive chef Gary Yin says leaders "help others to achieve success."

POWER SKILL: CONFLICT RESOLUTION

Disagreements happen. The key is knowing how to talk things through to find a fair solution. Say you're assigned a partner for a science project, but you quickly notice they don't seem interested in doing their fair share of the assignment. It might feel a little uncomfortable, but the right move is to stand up for yourself and respectfully address the issue so that your partner knows that their behavior is unacceptable. Grown-ups use this skill, too. HR managers help coworkers solve disputes. Diplomats work out peace agreements between countries. Documentary producer Mike Gunton helps solve conflicts between crew members on set; it's all in service of making a film turn out "as good as it possibly can," he says.

POWER SKILL: COLLABORATION

Collaboration means teaming up with others to get something done. It means doing your part while trusting others to do their part as well. Think of building a robot

with friends: one person codes, another designs, someone else tests. The same idea applies in a hospital, where doctors, nurses, and techs work together to care for a patient. Success depends on everyone. "One big thing for me is the team that I work with," says professional racing driver Jamie Chadwick. "When I see the effort and all the hard work that they put into trying to make me successful, that inspires me to be better daily."

Activity 5

Can you complete a power skills bingo board? Create a nine-box bingo card. Write one power skill in each square. (You can set the middle as a free space.) Over the next week, try to check off as many as you can by recognizing when you've used that skill. In a journal, jot down what you did to show each skill—whether it was organizing your desk or helping solve a group conflict. At the end of the week, reflect on your skills. Which came the most naturally? Which did you find yourself struggling with? Were you surprised by how often these power skills came up in your day-to-day life?

CHAPTER 5

OVERCOME OBSTACLES

Planning for your future career can be exciting, but the reality is that it won't always be easy. Questions will come up. Doubts can creep in. Life will throw you curveballs. You might find yourself thinking, *What if I can't figure this out? What if obstacles get in the way?*

"Career success requires the courage to go your own way and believe in yourself, even in tough times," writes career strategist Terina Allen. "The journey won't always be smooth. To be honest, you'll likely experience several bumps in the road as you work your way toward the job you want." When a potential problem comes up, know that you're not alone: Everyone experiences obstacles,

challenges, and doubts on their career journey. But these moments don't have to stop you in your tracks. Here are common "What if?" questions and ideas for addressing them.

WHAT IF I CAN'T DECIDE WHICH WAY TO GO?

That's totally normal, especially when you're young. Choosing a career doesn't happen all at once. You're allowed to explore and try different things. Follow your interests, learn what you can, and notice what feels exciting and what comes naturally to you. Every new experience teaches you something, even if it's "not this."

And remember, changing your mind or taking a detour is always an option. “It’s okay to change or expand your career aspirations, in increments large and small,” Allen writes. “It’s okay now and in the future.” (Yes, adults are allowed to change their minds, too!)

WHAT IF PRACTICAL THINGS, LIKE MONEY AND TIME, HOLD ME BACK?

Some dreams take extra time, effort, or resources. That’s just reality. It doesn’t mean a dream is impossible to reach; it means you need a plan.

Look for programs, scholarships, or groups that can help. Ask questions along the way. Don’t count out a nontraditional route: Kenashee Gumby became an urban composter after receiving money for school from an environmental nonprofit. Drew Masciotti’s night class at a local tech school turned into a successful career in welding and manufacturing. Some students who choose to pursue college degrees take part in work-study programs to help with tuition. The route you take to your career may end up including detours, and the path will probably not always be smooth. But with determination, creativity, and patience, you can find your way.

Many people work toward their goals in small steps. “Start where you are, with what you have,” advises DeVanté

Starks, of the Son of a Saint youth-development nonprofit program. "People sometimes feel like they aren't enough, or like they don't have enough. You can always work toward your goal or goals, no matter where you are or what you feel you lack."

WHAT IF THE CAREER PATH I WANT HAS NEVER BEEN TRAVELED BEFORE?

Then you might be the one to build it! Many careers today didn't exist a generation ago, or even a decade ago. If your goal is new or unusual, that's not a reason to quit. It's a reason to keep going. It might mean you'll need to invent part of the path; that takes courage, creativity, and

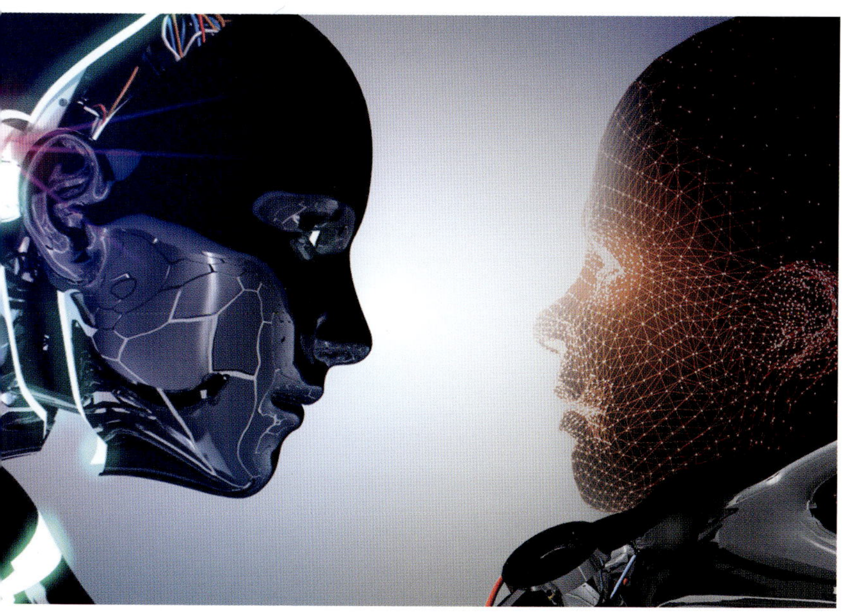

perseverance. Sometimes, being the first to do something can take extra work, but it's worth it to be able to have the career that feels best suited for you.

Technology is changing everything. That includes the kinds of careers people will have. The world will need people with a variety of strengths. It will need "the perspectives and approaches that come from diverse minds," says STEM advocate and senior IT specialist Beth Krawczuk. "Kids are in an amazing position to take advantage and continue to soar into the future." In other words? The future needs you, and whatever ideas you can dream up.

WHAT IF I HAVE TROUBLE BELIEVING IN MYSELF?

Self-doubt affects everyone. Even people you might consider to be extremely successful have doubted themselves. Along the way to becoming a professional soccer player, Bukayo Saka experienced days that made him wonder if he was good enough to succeed as a professional athlete. "There were some tough days," Saka says. "But you have to just keep going, keep dreaming, and keep believing."

When a doubting voice pops up in your head, try this: Forget the big picture. Focus instead on the next small step you can take. Then take it. Build your confidence through

action. “A great career starts with you,” writes Allen. “It starts with your belief in your potential.”

WHAT IF I FIND MYSELF FEELING OVERWHELMED OR DISAPPOINTED?

Disappointments can happen in any and every career path. It’s a risk, but it’s one worth taking. It’s okay to feel stuck, sad, or frustrated on your journey. This is where your support system comes in. “Sometimes your career goals will seem out of reach,” Allen writes. “Sometimes, life will get you down. When this happens, grab hold of the people who believe in you and your goals—your support system—and don’t let go.”

Talk to someone you trust. Take a break if you need to. Then try again, or try a new approach. Big goals take time, and nobody succeeds alone. Here's more advice, from CEO and education consultant Nadine Fonseca: "The reality is that your career adventure will rarely go exactly as you'd hoped," she writes. "Some things will turn out wildly better. Some will leave you frustrated and disappointed. And some will be fine but a bit different from what you expected."

Fonseca suggests embracing all of the emotions that come your way: "You won't be the first, or the last, person to feel discouraged *and* determined at the same time."

WHAT IF PEOPLE ARE PRESSURING ME TO TAKE A DIFFERENT PATH?

Sometimes friends or family think they're helping when they push a certain path. They might want you to be safe, be successful, or follow a family tradition. It's important to

listen to people you trust. It's also okay to make a different choice. Try to understand their point of view, then keep learning about what matters most to you. "Be prepared to demonstrate perseverance and courage as you overcome pressures from people along the way," Allen writes.

Activity 6

Write down three "What if?" questions that have crossed your mind when thinking about your future career. Then, brainstorm possible ways to respond to each potential obstacle. If you get stuck, ask a trusted adult for advice.

Activity 7

• • •

Think about a time you encountered an obstacle on your way toward a goal. What did you do? How did you feel as you were approaching it and after you overcame it? Did you rely on your support system or on any of your skills or talents?

CHAPTER 6

GO FORTH!

Congratulations! You've made it to the end of this book. But your career journey is just beginning. Whether you're already dreaming of a certain path or you're still figuring it out, you've taken the first step toward finding your way.

You've explored a wide range of industries, from technology and business to hospitality and personal service. You've seen how each career path is driven by people who follow their passions, use their unique skills, and make a difference in their communities. Remember how Terina Allen, the career strategist, shared her winding path? She didn't just wake up one day and know exactly what she wanted to do. She experimented, made choices, and grew through her experiences. She was open to whatever came next and embraced surprises. Your journey will likely have its own unexpected twists; that's part of the fun.

You've also learned that the world is constantly changing. New industries are emerging, and new jobs are being created every day. As technology continues to evolve, many jobs will shift, change, or disappear. As you continue

to build your skills, be ready to embrace change and seize opportunities when they arise.

What's next? It's time to take everything you've learned and start putting it into action. Review your Skills Explorer results. Set goals. Take risks. Ask questions. In the end, your career path isn't about choosing one job and sticking with it forever. It's about following the clues that lead you to your next step. Your journey may take you places you never expected.

The world needs your skills, your talents, and your passion. So go forth! Take the next step. Your future career path is yours to discover.

Tip: Find out more about the people and careers mentioned in this book at timeforkids.com/your-hot-job. Once you've signed up for a free account, with an adult's permission, you can take the virtual Skills Explorer quiz, dive into articles and videos, earn badges, and more. What are you waiting for?